The Rain Arrow

Written by Tony Mitton
Illustrated by Jane Johnson

Collins Educational

The hot plain was dry and dusty. No rain had come and the grass was brown and withered.

Koi-Kin was worried.
His cows might die of thirst and hunger.

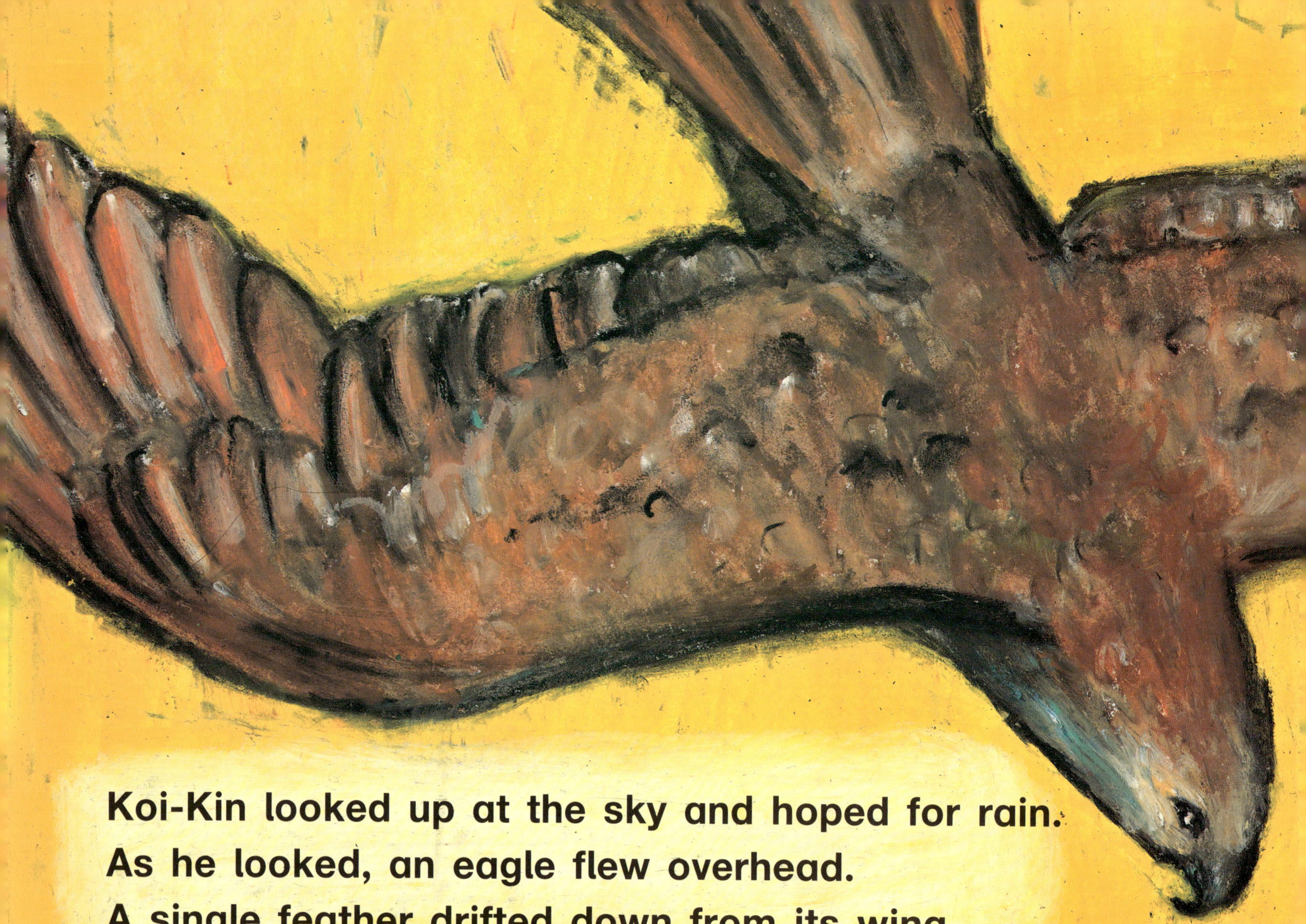

Koi-Kin looked up at the sky and hoped for rain.
As he looked, an eagle flew overhead.
A single feather drifted down from its wing.

Koi-Kin picked the feather up. Then he sharpened a stick and used the feather to make an arrow.

He fetched his bow from his hut.
Bending back and taking aim, he shot the arrow into the great, dark rain cloud overhead.

The cloud burst. With a loud rumble,
the rain came pouring down.
The thirsty ground drank the water up gratefully.

Soon the plain was soft and green again,
and Koi-Kin's cows grew fat and happy once more.

As Koi-Kin stood watching his herd,
he saw the eagle fly overhead.
Koi-Kin smiled and waved his hand in thanks.